University
of Worcester

Information & Learning Services

**Peirson Building, Henwick Grove, St John's, Worcester
WR2 6AJ Telephone: 01905 855341**

Return on or before the last date stamped below

RENEW ONLINE @ http://login.worc.ac.uk

Colours in Nature

Blue

Lisa Bruce

Heinemann
LIBRARY

Little Nippers

www.heinemann.co.uk/library

Visit our website to find out more information about **Heinemann Library** books.

To order:
☎ Phone 44 (0) 1865 888066
▤ Send a fax to 44 (0) 1865 314091
▣ Visit the Heinemann Bookshop at www.heinemann.co.uk/library to browse our catalogue and order online.

First published in Great Britain by Heinemann Library, Halley Court, Jordan Hill, Oxford OX2 8EJ, part of Harcourt Education.
Heinemann is a registered trademark of Harcourt Education Ltd.

Editorial: Jilly Attwood and Claire Throp
Design: Jo Hinton-Malivoire and bigtop, Bicester, UK
Models made by: Jo Brooker
Picture Research: Catherine Bevan
Production: Séverine Ribierre

Originated by Dot Gradations
Printed and bound in China by South China Printing Company

ISBN 0 431 17231 5 (hardback)
07 06 05 04 03
10 9 8 7 6 5 4 3 2 1

ISBN 0 431 17236 6 (paperback)
07 06 05 04 03
10 9 8 7 6 5 4 3 2 1

British Library Cataloguing in Publication Data
Bruce, Lisa
Blue – (Colours in nature)
535.6
A full catalogue record for this book is available from the British Library.

Acknowledgements
The publishers would like to thank the following for permission to reproduce photographs:
Ardea pp. **16** (J. L. Mason), **21** (P. Morris); Bruce Coleman pp. **6** (Christer Fredriksson), **17** (Kim Taylor); Corbis p. **13**; Imagestate p. **19**; KPT Power Photos p. **10–11**; Nature Picture Library p. **14–15**; Peter Evans p. **23**; Photodisc pp. **7**, **8**, **9**, **18**; Robert Harding pp. **20**, **22**; SPL pp. **4–5** (Sinclair Stammers), **12** (Geoff Bryant)

Cover photograph reproduced with permission of Photodisc

The publishers would like to thank Annie Davy for her assistance in the preparation of this book.

Every effort has been made to contact copyright holders of any material reproduced in this book. Any omissions will be rectified in subsequent printings if notice is given to the publishers.

2

Contents

Blue in nature

Nature is full of wonderful colours.

What can you think of in nature that is blue?

Blue waters

There is a lot of blue water in our world.

Rivers and lakes look blue.

Blue sea

Dark blue sea

Light blue sea

Blue sky

Way up high the sky is blue.

Is it light blue or dark blue?

Blue flowers

Some flowers
have blue petals

These bluebells look like a blue carpet in the wood.

Blue animals

The blue whale lives in the sea.

14

It is the
BIGGEST
animal in the world.

Blue insects

The damselfly is brilliant blue.

The bluebottle fly is dark blue.

17

Blue birds

This peacock is bright blue.

The kingfisher swoops and dives for fish in the river.

His feathers are a shiny blue.

Blue fish

This fish is shiny blue.

How many fish
can you see?

Changing colour

On a rainy day the sky is grey.

When the Sun comes out the sky changes to bright blue.

23

Index

The end

Notes for adults

This series supports young children's knowledge and understanding of the world around them. The four books will help to form the foundation for later work in science and geography. The following Early Learning Goals are relevant to this series:
- begin to differentiate colours
- explore what happens when they mix colours
- find out about and identify some features of living things, objects and events they observe
- look closely at similarities, differences, patterns and change
- ask questions about why things happen and how things work
- observe, find out about and identify features in the places they live and the natural world
- find out about their environment, and talk about those features they like and dislike.

The *Colours in Nature* series introduces children to colours and their different shades by exploring features of the natural world. It will also help children to think more about living things and life processes, which may lead on to discussion of environmental issues. The children should be encouraged to be aware of the weather and seasonal changes and how these affect the place in which they live.

This book will help children extend their vocabulary, as they will hear new words such as petals, bluebells, whale, damselfly, bluebottle fly, peacock and kingfisher.

Additional information

The male common blue damselfly (page16) is typically blue and black. The usual female form is dark with dull green replacing the blue areas of the male. The blue tang (page 20) is a member of the surgeonfish family. They have sharp, movable spines on each side of the tail that resemble a surgeon's scalpel. Young fishes are bright yellow, but by adulthood they are a deep, rich blue all over.

Follow-up activities

Using blue paper or material, create a river effect across the floor. Ask the children to cut out fish shapes from card on to which paper clips are attached. Make a fishing rod utilising a small magnet as the hook. See how many fish the children can catch.

Sing nursery rhymes with a blue theme such as 'Lavender blue'.